Rugby

Clive Gifford

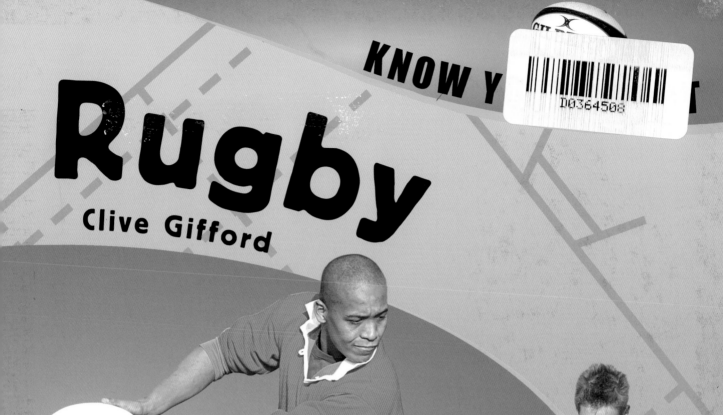

FRANKLIN WATTS
LONDON · SYDNEY

D0364508

First published in 2006 by
Franklin Watts
338 Euston Road
London NW1 3BH

Franklin Watts Australia
Hachette Children's Books
Level 17/207 Kent Street
Sydney NSW 2000

© Franklin Watts 2006
Series editor: Jennifer Schofield
Art director: Jonathan Hair

**Series designed and created for
Franklin Watts by Painted Fish Ltd.**
Designer: Rita Storey
Editor: Nicola Edwards
Photography: Tudor Photography,
   Banbury

A CIP catalogue record
for this book is available
from the British Library.

Dewey classification: 796.333
ISBN-10: 0 7496 6464 9
ISBN-13: 978 07496 6464 0
Printed in China

Note: At the time of going to press, the statistics
and player profiles in this book were up to date.
However, due to some players' active participation
in the sport, it is possible that some of these may
now be out of date.

Picture credits
Action plus/Neil Tingle p.6; Action plus/
Steve Bardens p.7; Action plus/Glyn Kirk
p.9; Action plus/Steve Bardens p.11;
Action plus/Andrew Cornaga p.21; Action
plus/Neil Tingle p.22; Action plus/Neil
Tingle p.25; Action plus/Glyn Kirk p.26;
Action plus/Neil Tingle p. 27.

Cover images: Tudor Photography,
Banbury.

All photos posed by models.
Thanks to Joel Avery, Tim Bennett,
Carl Daniels, Josh Deegan, Carl Taylor
and Mark Woodward.

The Publisher would like to thank Banbury
RUFC for the use of the club's ground.

Taking part in sport
is a fun way to get fit, but
like any form of physical
exercise it has an element of
risk, particularly if you are unfit,
overweight or suffer from any
medical conditions. It is advisable
to consult a healthcare
professional before beginning
any programme
of exercise.

Contents

ST. COLUMBA'S HIGH SCHOOL
LIBRARY
CLYDEBANK

Introduction

Rugby is a tough, all-action game played between two teams. It is great to watch and even more fun to play. It comes in many versions but all versions feature an oval ball which players carry in their hands, pass or kick. The two teams try to score points while preventing their opponents from scoring points against them.

Aim of the Game

The two teams try to gain points by scoring 'tries'. A try is scored when a player grounds the ball in the in-goal area (see page 8) of the opposing team. When a team scores a try it has the chance to add extra points by kicking the ball between the goalposts. This is called a 'conversion'. Teams can also score points through penalty kicks and drop goals.

The Birth of Rugby

Teams in the men's World Cup compete for the William Webb Ellis Trophy. It is named after a pupil at Rugby School, in England, who was playing a game of football in 1823 when he picked up the ball and ran with it in his hands. Many believe this was how rugby began.

Kenny Logan scores a try for Scotland. In rugby union, a try is worth five points. Kicking the conversion earns a further two points.

6

Rugby for All

Rugby union is open to players of all shapes and sizes. It is also played at all age and ability levels. Many rugby clubs run teams ranging from under-10s to over-40s. Women's and girls' rugby is also booming in popularity. For the world's best players, the most important competition is the World Cup, which is held separately for men and women. It is played every four years.

Junior Games

Rugby union is a 15-a-side game played over two halves of 40 minutes each. Smaller-scale versions of the game, played for shorter times and featuring fewer players, exist for younger players. These include tag rugby, which is a non-contact version of the sport, and mini rugby. In some countries, girls and boys play mini and tag rugby together until the age of 11.

The History of Rugby

In the 19th century, different versions of football and rugby football emerged. In 1871, clubs met to draw up an agreed way of playing and formed the Rugby Football Union. Arguments about professionalism (being paid to play) raged within the Union and in 1895, 21 rugby clubs in the north of England broke away to form the Northern Football League, which was later renamed the Rugby Football League. Both Union and League have developed different rules and ways of playing (see pages 24–27). This book concentrates on rugby union.

In tag rugby, a player is 'tackled' when an opponent manages to pull away a ribbon from the player's belt. The tackler then steps back and the tackled player must pass the ball.

Players, Pitch and Positions

A full-sized rugby pitch is up to 69 metres wide and 100 metres long, with two in-goal areas of a maximum depth of 22 metres. The 15 players on each side are divided into eight forwards (the players who form scrums – see page 26) and seven backs.

Referees and Rules

The referee is in charge of the rugby match and makes decisions that have to be followed by all the players. The referee is assisted by two touch judges. They run up and down the touchline during the game and also stand beneath the goalposts when a penalty kick or conversion is taken. In some top-flight rugby league and union games, there is an additional official, known as the video referee. When a try is in dispute, for example, the match referee can signal to the video referee to give a ruling.

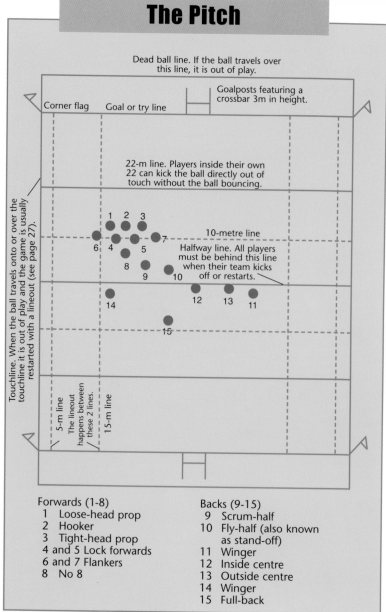

The Pitch

Dead ball line. If the ball travels over this line, it is out of play.

Goalposts featuring a crossbar 3m in height.

Corner flag   Goal or try line

22-m line. Players inside their own 22 can kick the ball directly out of touch without the ball bouncing.

10-metre line

Halfway line. All players must be behind this line when their team kicks off or restarts.

Touchline. When the ball travels onto or over the touchline it is out of play and the game is usually restarted with a lineout (see page 27).

5-m line

The lineout happens between these 2 lines.

15-m line

Forwards (1-8)
1   Loose-head prop
2   Hooker
3   Tight-head prop
4 and 5 Lock forwards
6 and 7 Flankers
8   No 8

Backs (9-15)
9   Scrum-half
10 Fly-half (also known as stand-off)
11 Winger
12 Inside centre
13 Outside centre
14 Winger
15 Full-back

The Referee's Signals

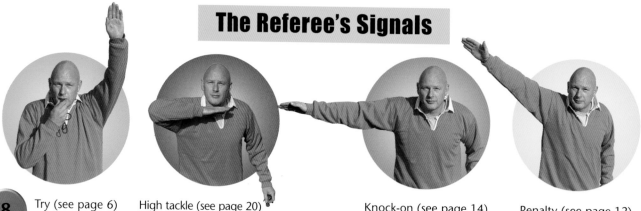

Try (see page 6)   High tackle (see page 20)   Knock-on (see page 14)   Penalty (see page 12)

The scrum-half is the link between the forwards and the backs. Here, scrum half Steve So'oialo has collected the ball from a scrum and is passing to the backs.

Rugby is a technical game with many complicated rules. Players need to learn all the laws of rugby. You should discuss any you are unsure about with your coach.

Forwards and Backs

Forwards are involved in scrums and lineouts (see pages 26–27) and generally in winning the ball for their side. They feed the ball to the scrum-half and fly-half who have the choice of kicking the ball, running with it or passing it out to the backs. Forwards tend to be larger, heavier and slower than backs, though the difference between them is becoming less and less in modern rugby. This can be seen at the highest level, where forwards need to be able to move around the pitch quickly, while backs need to be strong enough to surge through tackles and defend well.

Restarts

Each half of a match is started with a kick-off taken from the centre spot. Kick-offs are also used to restart the game after a try is scored. The ball must travel over the opponents' 10-m line and stay in play. If not, the opposing team can order the kick to be re-taken or it can choose to have a scrum (see page 26) on the centre spot. Another type of restart, the 22-m drop out, is a drop kick (see page 22) taken from behind the 22-m line.

Sin Bin

If a player is guilty of foul play such as fighting, stamping on an opponent or persistently breaking rules, a referee may send a player to the 'sin bin'. The player is sent off the field and cannot return or be substituted for ten minutes.

An Unusual Incident

The legendary New Zealand player George Nepia was involved in a charity match when the ball came to him. He scooped it up and scored a try. The only problem was that he was refereeing the match!

Training and Kit

Rugby union is fast and physical. Players need to be very fit to perform at their best. Rugby can also be a dangerous game. To avoid injury, players need to prepare for matches thoroughly and always obey the referee's instructions.

A Player's Kit

Players in the same team wear identical strips. Rugby shirts and shorts tend to be made of hard-wearing cotton. Keeping your shirt tucked into your shorts is not just a matter of smartness but it also gives less material for an opponent to grab hold of. Long socks are held up by elastic or garters. Boots (ideally with adjustable screw-in studs) should fit comfortably and laces should be securely tied. A tracksuit to keep warm before and after a game is also important.

Protection

Added protection is a matter of personal choice. For instance, some players choose to wear lightweight, football-style shinpads to protect the front of their legs. Some players protect their head and ears by wearing a padded headguard, called a scrum cap. It is a good idea to wear a correctly sized gumshield during games.

Stretching Exercises

Rugby players perform a series of stretches to the key muscles in their legs, arms and back before starting a game. These stretches help them perform at their best and help prevent injuries.

Preparation

Rugby players use a whole range of muscles during a match, from reaching up to take a high ball (see page 15) to stretching down or diving low to score a try or collect the ball on the ground. They need to prepare their whole body before matches to avoid injury and to play at their best. Players often warm up before a match with some running, star jumps and other exercises, as well as a series of stretches to their upper and lower leg, groin, back, shoulder and neck muscles.

Skills and Fitness

Adult players can do weight training in the gym to help build muscle and strength. Junior players need to concentrate on developing their fitness and skills. Fitness can be improved by playing other physical sports, such as football, training regularly and eating healthily. Some basic skills such as passing and catching and swerves and sidesteps (see pages 12–15 and 18–19) can be practised with a couple of friends in a park.

Many injuries occur during tackles, especially if a player tackles with poor technique. This young player is practising using a safe tackle bag under the watchful eye of his coach.

Jonah Lomu

Date of birth: May 12th, 1975

Nationality: New Zealander

Position: Winger

Height: 1.96m

Weight: approximately 120kg

International caps: 73

Points: 215

Jonah Lomu became the youngest player to play for New Zealand's All Blacks, when he made his debut in 1994. A year later, he was the star of the 1995 World Cup, where he scored seven tries. He followed that at the 1999 World Cup with eight tries. Incredibly strong and powerful, Lomu is also a very quick runner, capable of running 100m in 10.8 seconds. Battling against a serious kidney illness, Lomu had to have a kidney transplant in 2004. However, he made a comeback in late 2005 and hopes to play in the 2007 World Cup.

Passing

Passing links a team's play together. The ball must be thrown backwards or sideways but never forward, which is against the rules. If a player deliberately passes the ball forward, the referee may award a penalty. If it is thrown forward accidentally, the referee orders a scrum (see page 26) at the place where the pass was made.

The Lateral Pass

This is the most basic and the most common pass in rugby and is an essential part of every rugby player's skills. Top players continue to practise their passing throughout their careers. Accuracy is very important. When you and the person receiving the pass are moving forwards, you have to judge where the receiver will be by the time the pass arrives. You should make that your target, aiming the ball so that the receiver catches the ball at chest height. The ball needs to be thrown with the right amount of force and the timing of the pass is crucial.

The Lateral Pass

1 The player looks for the person to whom he is passing. He holds the ball at chest height in both hands. Only his fingers are in contact with the surface of the ball.

2 The passer swings his arms across his body towards the receiver. His rear hand pushes the ball while the other hand guides it in the right direction.

3 As the ball leaves his hands, the passer flicks his wrists and fingers. This puts some spin on the ball, which helps it to fly directly towards the target. The player follows through with his arms and fingers pointing towards the target.

The passer (left) keeps an eye on both his receiver (far right) and the opponent closing in. He must time his pass well.

An Olympic Sport

The USA remain reigning Olympic rugby union champions. Rugby Union appeared in four Olympics, the last being won by the USA in 1924.

Long and Short

The lateral pass can be thrown long or short. To throw a short 'pop' pass, hold the ball at about chest height and flick your fingers and wrists to send the ball up and towards the receiver. To send a long lateral pass you need to swing your shoulders and twist at the waist to add power. A good, long pass can open up a game and release players in plenty of space to run forward. There is a risk that the ball might be intercepted by an opponent, so throw a long pass only if there is space and you are confident of your accuracy.

Passing Drills

Passing and catching cannot be practised enough. Many beginners find it far easier to pass in one direction than the other. Players should work hard on their weaker side so that they can pass from either hand. A good drill is for three players to stand in a row a few metres apart and to run and pass the ball back and forth. The player in the middle has to pass and receive the ball in both directions. Repeat this drill several times, switching over the player in the middle.

Corridor Drill

Alternatively, in an area, or 'corridor', 10–12m wide, two players must repeatedly pass the ball to each other, making sure not to pass the ball forward. The defender cannot tackle the players but can try to intercept the ball. If the ball is intercepted, dropped or goes outside the corridor, the defender changes places with one of the passers. Walk through this drill a few times before gradually building up speed.

Catching

Catching the ball is just as important as passing it. If you fail to catch the ball, your opponents may gain possession, putting your team in danger of conceding a try.

Knock-on

A fumbled catch may result in the referee signalling a 'knock-on'. This is when a player fails to catch the ball and fumbles it forward so that it touches the ground.

When this happens, a referee will award a scrum (see page 26) to the opposing team. It is not a knock-on if a player fumbles the ball but catches it at the second attempt before it touches the ground.

Safe Hands

Always stay alert so that you are ready to receive a pass at any time. If possible, try to take the catch with two hands and then pull the ball into your body to protect it.

◄ Always be prepared for a ball that does not arrive at the ideal height. You may have to bend and stretch to catch a low ball or reach up high.

Catching

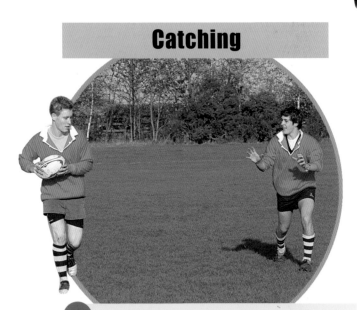

1 *The receiver is in a position to receive a pass, his eyes are focused on the passer. When the ball is released, the receiver's hands are at chest height, with his thumbs up and fingers spread. This helps create a target for the pass.*

2 *The receiver keeps his eyes on the ball. As the pass arrives, the player extends his hands towards the ball without over-stretching. He gets a good grip on the ball and brings his hands in and down to cushion its landing.*

Taking a High Ball on the Ground

1 The player calls to his team-mates that he is going to take the catch. Keeping his eyes on the ball, he gets into position to catch it. He spreads his feet apart to help his balance and raises his arms, fingers spread and pointing upwards.

2 As the player catches the ball, he cushions it by bringing his arms down towards his chest. The player crouches and turns his body to protect the ball from approaching opponents.

In the Air

Sometimes you may need to jump to catch a high ball. You cannot be tackled while you are in the air. If an opponent tries to tackle you when your feet are off the ground, the referee should award your team a penalty. If you catch the ball in your own 22-metre area, you can call a 'mark' – literally by shouting 'mark!' as you catch it. When you do this, the players in the other team have to retreat 10m, your team-mates fall in behind you and you are awarded a free-kick.

Ball-handling

As part of their preparation before a game, players practise passing and catching to get a feel for the ball. This is especially important if the conditions are wet or windy, the pitch is greasy, which can make the ball slippery, or if it is very cold. You can practise some elements of ball-handling by yourself. Throw the ball up and over to one side of your shoulders and then twist at the waist to collect it securely at chest height. Throw the ball higher and straight up and get underneath it to practise your high catching.

15

Timing Runs

Instead of kicking or passing the ball, players may see some space ahead and decide to run with the ball themselves. Players need to know when and how to make attacking runs with the ball and, importantly, how to support their team's attack by making runs without the ball.

Running with the Ball

Every running situation in a rugby match is different, but there are key things you should do every time you run with the ball. You should always protect the ball by keeping it close to your chest. Keep your head up and be aware of how play is developing around you. Has a gap appeared? Are opponents closing in? Is there a team-mate in a better position to whom you can pass? Should you kick ahead or into touch? These are decisions you have to make while running hard.

This player has his head up and his eyes focused on a gap into which he wants to sprint. He holds the ball securely in both hands.

Supporting Runs

The player with the ball is called the ball-carrier. Good teams try to not let their ball-carrier become isolated on the pitch. If the ball-carrier is about to be tackled, team-mates offer support and give the player options for a pass. If tackled, they will also offer support to try to keep possession of the ball. In attack, team-mates try to make runs at different angles to split and disrupt the other team's defence.

Overlap Play

Through passing and running with the ball, teams seek to create an attacking situation where they have more players ready to receive the ball than there are defenders to guard or tackle them. One example of this is the overlap.

A Unique Player

Thomas Gordon won three caps for Ireland over 100 years ago. It makes him the only one-handed player to play in an international match.

The Overlap

1 The ball-carrier runs hard but is aware of a defender closing in on him. Meanwhile, his team-mate is starting a fast run down the touchline to create an overlap.

2 The defender is caught in two minds over whether to tackle the ball-carrier or to follow the wide runner. The ball-carrier waits for the right moment to pass. If it is too late, the receiver may be ahead of him. If it is too early, the defender may anticipate the pass and intercept the ball.

3 The defender has been drawn towards the ball-carrier, who releases the pass at the right moment. The receiver collects the pass and is free to run down the touchline.

17

Beating an Opponent

The easiest way to beat an opponent is to pass the ball to a team-mate. There are some situations where you need to keep hold of the ball and go past an opponent on your own. When it is done well, beating an opponent by using speed and surprise is one of the most exhilarating moments in rugby.

Change of Pace and Direction

Changes of pace and direction are simple but effective ways of getting past an opponent. A decrease in your running speed, together with a slight change of direction in your running line, may cause a defender to hesitate and give you the chance to sprint away from them at full speed.

The Swerve

Harder to learn, the swerve is a more dramatic change of direction. For a simple swerve, approach the defender straight on with the ball in both hands. Three or four paces before you reach the defender, lean sharply to one side and make your next stride across your body. Use the edges of your boots to lean away and swerve around the player. As soon as you are clear of the defender, sprint away as straight and as fast as you can.

The Dummy Move

A dummy is when you pretend to pass to a team-mate to fool one or more defenders but actually keep hold of the ball. For it to work well your movements have to be convincing and there has to be a team-mate in close support.

The Dummy

1 *If the defender does not commit to tackling the ball-carrier, the ball-carrier turns his head to his team-mate and goes through all the movements of making a pass but keeps a firm grip on the ball.*

2 *The defender is deceived into believing that the ball-carrier is about to pass and makes a move to tackle his team-mate. The ball-carrier quickly changes his running angle away from the defender and increases his pace to sprint away.*

The Sidestep

A sidestep can also be used to get past an opponent. To perform a sidestep, this player puts all his weight on his right foot and then drives off that foot to change direction towards his left. Performed well, a sidestep can fool a defender into moving in the wrong direction.

The Scissors or Switch Pass

Another way that two team-mates can beat a defender is the scissors pass. The player with the ball changes their running line to move diagonally across the pitch. Their team-mate changes their running line, too, running in the opposite diagonal direction behind them. Just before the two cross, the ball-carrier twists at the waist so that they are facing backwards and releases a short, gentle pass. The receiver collects the ball and sprints away.

The Scissors or Switch Pass

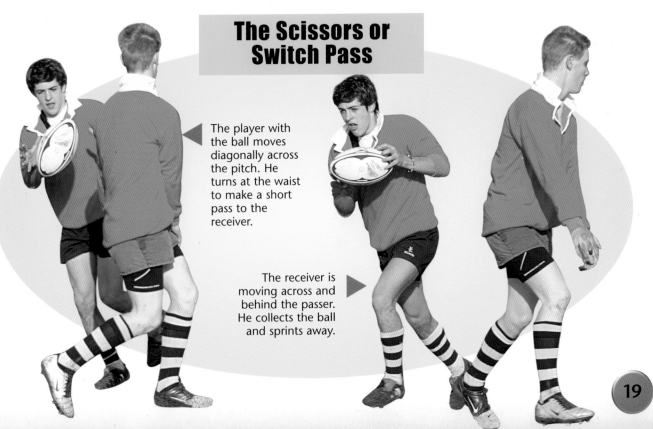

The player with the ball moves diagonally across the pitch. He turns at the waist to make a short pass to the receiver.

The receiver is moving across and behind the passer. He collects the ball and sprints away.

Tackling

Tackling is a key part of defence. It should be practised often, under the supervision of your coach. Tackling with the correct technique will result in fewer injuries.

Tackle Talk

Tackling is more about skill and technique than brute strength. Good technique will allow smaller players to tackle bigger and heavier players. Apart from learning tackling techniques, players must know the rules about tackling. For example, you should never stick out a foot to trip an opponent or make a high tackle around the neck or head. Both are against the rules of rugby and could be very dangerous. Nor should you make a late tackle, where you tackle a player who does not have the ball.

Side-on Tackle

The side-on tackle is one of the most common tackles in a game. Many coaches of junior players believe that it is also the best tackle to learn first.

The Side-on Tackle

1 *The tackler focuses on the opponent with the ball, aiming to make contact just above waist height. This is where his shoulder will impact with the player.*

2 *The tackler drives off on the leg on the same side of the body as the shoulder making the impact. He uses his full body weight to hit his opponent. He must make sure that his head slips behind the player being tackled and not in front. This helps avoid injuries.*

Beaten?

If your opponent gets past you, do not give up but sprint back hard. A team-mate may have slowed down his attack and you could be needed to help out or make another tackle. A tap tackle can be used when an opponent is out of reach of a full tackle. Use an outstretched arm to give one of your opponent's ankles a firm tap. This can knock a player off balance or cause them to stumble and fall.

Defending

There is more to defending than just tackling. All the players in a team should defend as a single unit. They should spread out across the pitch to protect their territory and their try line. Defenders look to cut down the space the ball-carrier and his supporting team-mates have. Defenders must also stay alert to opponents running into danger areas or an unexpected kick above or behind them.

Serge Betsen

Date of birth: March 25th, 1974

Nationality: French

Position: Flanker

Height: 1.82m

Weight: 96kg

International caps: 48

Points: 45

Nicknamed the Biarritz Bombshell, Betsen is known as one of the most ferocious and frequent tacklers in the game. He helped inspire France to win both the 2002 and 2004 Six Nations competitions. He also has an eye for attack, having scored nine tries for the French national team.

3 *As he makes impact, the tackler wraps his arms around his opponent's legs and holds firmly. He and his opponent fall to the ground.*

Kicking

There are many types of kick in rugby union. Some are to score points, such as the penalty kick or the drop kick aimed between the posts. Other kicks are used to improve a team's position, to set up an attack or to clear the ball into touch.

Drop Kicks

Drop kicks are used for some restarts and when trying to score a drop goal (when a player kicks the ball over the crossbar and between the posts). To perform a drop kick, begin with the ball in your hands. Then release or drop the ball and as it touches the ground, swing your foot through the ball, finishing with a high follow-through. It is important to keep your head down, your eyes on the ball and your weight on your non-kicking foot. You can take turns to practise drop kicks with a friend standing on the opposite side of the posts.

Jonny Wilkinson

Date of birth: May 25th, 1979

Nationality: English

Position: Fly-half (occasionally, centre)

Height: 1.78m

Weight: 85kg

International caps: 52

International points: 817

Wilkinson will always be remembered for his drop kick in the last minute of extra time against Australia that won England the 2003 World Cup. He is England's leading all-time points-scorer but is more than just a phenomenally accurate goalkicker. He is deceptively quick, an astute passer and a ferocious tackler. A long-serving member of the Newcastle Falcons club, he suffered from numerous injury problems after the 2003 World Cup. He recovered to be selected for the 2005 British and Irish Lions tour of New Zealand but struggled to rediscover his old form.

The Drop Kick

In a drop kick, the kicker aims to make contact a third of the way from the bottom of the ball just as it reaches the ground. This should lift the ball high into the air.

Goal Kick

1 With the ball pointing upwards or lined up towards the target on a mound of dirt or plastic kicking tee, the kicker starts his approach. His head is down and his eyes are focused on the ball.

2 The kicker places his non-kicking foot 10–20cm to the side of the ball and slightly behind it. He supports his bodyweight on this leg and keeps his head over the ball as his kicking leg swings through the ball.

3 The instep (where the boot laces are) makes contact about a third of the way up the ball. The kicker's leg follows through in front and slightly across his body.

Goalkicking

Goalkicking is used for conversions and for penalty kicks. All goalkickers have their own way of lining up a kick and how many paces they take to the ball. Work with your coach to find out what suits you best.

Grubber Kicks

The grubber kick is a low, stabbed or punched kick that causes the ball to roll end over end along the ground. It can be used to put the ball into touch when outside of the 22–m area and to nudge the ball forward and past the opposition defence for a team-mate to sprint onto and collect. Make sure your body is over the ball and aim for your laces to hit the upper half of the ball, keeping your leg low and straight in the follow-through.

Punts and Other Kicks

Other kicks used in rugby union include the long punt, which is often used by a fly-half or full-back to kick the ball into touch. It is similar to a drop kick, but the player's boot makes contact with the ball before the ball touches the ground. There is also the high kick, known as a garryowen or an up-and-under. This is kicked in a similar way to the punt but hoisted high into the air. The aim is to put the opposition team under pressure as you and your team-mates chase down the kick.

Rugby league and rugby union differ in a number of ways, such as the number of players in each team and the rules about tackling.

After the Tackle: Rugby Union

When a player is tackled in rugby union, a complicated set of rules applies. The tackled player must let go of the ball but will try to turn and place it so that a team-mate can collect it. A ruck occurs when the ball is on the ground and competing players from both teams are in physical contact. In a ruck, only players on their feet can handle the ball. When the ball is trapped under a pile of bodies, both teams will try to drive forward to release the ball and gain possession.

Key Rule Differences

	Rugby League	Rugby Union
Number of players	13	15
Points for a try	4	5
Points for a drop goal	1	3
Points for a penalty kick	2	3
Numbers of players in scrum	6	8

Collecting the Ball: Rugby Union

▲ The tackled player has managed to turn back facing his try line and places the ball at arm's length. His supporting team-mate is the first to arrive. He steps over the ball and bends his knees to get low as he collects the ball.

Mauls: Rugby Union

A maul is another move which can occur after a tackle. A maul can form when a player has been tackled but keeps hold of the ball, is in physical contact with an opponent, stays on his feet and is joined by supporting team-mates who must join from behind. These players maintain contact and try to drive forward, staying on their feet until either a player with the ball breaks away or a pass is made.

After the Tackle: Rugby League

In rugby league, a tackler must get off the player they have tackled as quickly as possible, otherwise a penalty may be awarded by the referee. The tackled player must then play the ball. This is done by placing the ball on the ground and rolling it backwards with a foot to a team-mate behind. The team-mate can then pick up the ball and play it.

Six Tackles: Rugby League

When players from the same team are tackled six times in a row, possession of the ball then passes to the opposing team. Teams try to drive up the pitch in the early phase of a set of six tackles. As the sixth tackle approaches, a team will often kick the ball deep into the other team's half to gain territorial advantage. If they are near the opponents' try line when the sixth tackle approaches, they may continue running and passing. Another option is a short kick into their opponents' in-goal area in the hope of scoring a try.

Willie Poching of the Leeds Rhinos is tackled by two Canterbury Bulldogs players during a rugby league game. The referee will indicate when a tackle is made. At that point, one player can stand in front of the tackled player. The other opponents have to retreat 5 metres.

After a tackle is completed in rugby league, the tackled player can roll the ball back to a team-mate using the sole of his boot.

25

The different codes of rugby have different ways of restarting the game after it has been stopped. In rugby union, two of these restarts, the scrum and the lineout, form important parts of the game.

Scrums: Rugby Union

In a rugby union scrum, eight forwards line up in a 3-2-3 formation, binding together in set ways. On the referee's signal, the two sets of forwards lock together, or 'engage'. The scrum-half from one of the two teams feeds the ball down the tunnel between the two front rows. His hooker aims to strike the ball, rolling it back to the feet of the No 8, the player at the back of the scrum. This player controls the ball with his feet. He can keep it under control as the scrum moves forward, pick it up and run with it or let it out of the scrum for his scrum-half to pick up and pass.

Scrums: Rugby League

In rugby league, when the ball goes out from the touchline, a scrum is taken level with where the ball went out of touch. A scrum may also be awarded when a team knocks on or throws a forward pass. The rugby league scrum lines up with three in the front row, two in the second and one in the third. The ball is fed in by the scrum-half and the middle player in the front row tries to hook (strike) the ball backwards. Scrums can be dangerous because of the enormous weight and power involved. Never practise scrums without an experienced coach on hand.

Australian scrum-half George Gregan passes the ball away from his forwards during an international rugby union match against Scotland.

Lineouts: Rugby Union

Lineouts occur only in rugby union. They take place when the ball crosses the touchline and goes out of play. The team that did not touch the ball last throws the ball in at the lineout. An exception is when a team is awarded a penalty and kicks the ball into touch. In this case, the kicking team gets the throw-in. Up to seven forwards from each team line up between 5 and 15 metres from the touchline. The throw-in is taken by the hooker, who judges the length, height and timing of his throw so that his team's jumpers have the best chance of reaching the ball before their opponents. The throw must be straight, or the referee will halt play. The jumpers may catch the ball or knock it back to their scrum-half.

Wendell Sailor

Date of Birth: July 16th, 1974

Nationality: Australian

Position: Winger

Height 1.91m

Weight: 106kg

International caps: 37

Points: 65

Australia's Wendell Sailor was one of rugby's union's most successful converts from rugby league where he scored an astonishing 110 tries in 189 club games for the Brisbane Broncos. Making the switch in codes in 2001, Sailor's mixture of power and pace has seen him disrupt many defences and produce tries for himself and team-mates.

Ian Gough of Wales and Bakkies Botha of South Africa leap high to win the ball from a lineout. Both players are supported in their jump by their team-mates.

Statistics and Records

Rugby Union

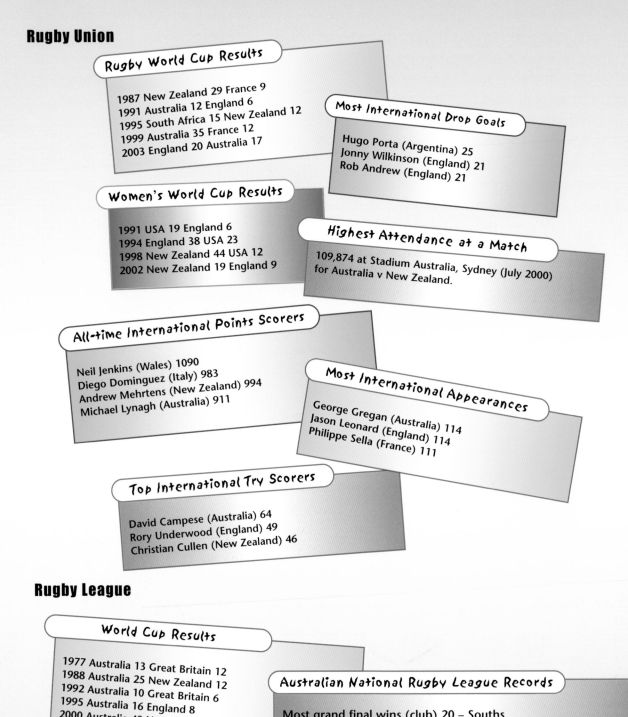

Rugby World Cup Results

1987 New Zealand 29 France 9
1991 Australia 12 England 6
1995 South Africa 15 New Zealand 12
1999 Australia 35 France 12
2003 England 20 Australia 17

Most International Drop Goals

Hugo Porta (Argentina) 25
Jonny Wilkinson (England) 21
Rob Andrew (England) 21

Women's World Cup Results

1991 USA 19 England 6
1994 England 38 USA 23
1998 New Zealand 44 USA 12
2002 New Zealand 19 England 9

Highest Attendance at a Match

109,874 at Stadium Australia, Sydney (July 2000) for Australia v New Zealand.

All-time International Points Scorers

Neil Jenkins (Wales) 1090
Diego Dominguez (Italy) 983
Andrew Mehrtens (New Zealand) 994
Michael Lynagh (Australia) 911

Most International Appearances

George Gregan (Australia) 114
Jason Leonard (England) 114
Philippe Sella (France) 111

Top International Try Scorers

David Campese (Australia) 64
Rory Underwood (England) 49
Christian Cullen (New Zealand) 46

Rugby League

World Cup Results

1977 Australia 13 Great Britain 12
1988 Australia 25 New Zealand 12
1992 Australia 10 Great Britain 6
1995 Australia 16 England 8
2000 Australia 40 New Zealand 12

Australian National Rugby League Records

Most grand final wins (club) 20 – Souths
Most grand final wins (individual) 10 – Norm Provan
Leading points-scorer in a season: 342 – Hazem El Masri (2004)

28

Glossary

Backs The seven players who line up behind the scrum.

Ball-carrier The player holding the ball.

Conversion A kick awarded after a try. The ball must travel between the posts and over the crossbar. A successful conversion is worth two points in rugby union and in rugby league.

Drop kick A kick where the ball is dropped and kicked as it lands on the ground.

Dummy pass Pretending to make a pass by going right through the passing movement but retaining the ball and aiming to send the defender the wrong way.

Forward pass A pass that is thrown forward to another player.

Forwards The eight players who form scrums and contest lineouts.

Knock-on When the ball touches the hand or arm of a player and is knocked forward and touches the ground.

Lineout A set piece where forwards line up in parallel lines and the ball is thrown in from the touchline for players to catch or knock back to their scrum-half.

Overlap An attacking situation where attackers outnumber defenders.

Possession Having the ball under control.

Scrum A set piece where usually eight players a side (six in rugby league) link together.

Sidestep A sudden change of forward direction used by the ball-carrier to get past a defender.

Tackle Grabbing hold of the player with the ball so that they are brought to the ground.

Tap tackle A firm tap of the opponent's ankles by a defender's hand.

Touchline The lines marking the side edges of the pitch.

Try A scoring move worth five points in rugby union and four in rugby league.

Websites

www.irb.com
The official website of the International Rugby Board, the organization that runs international rugby, including the World Cup. You can download a copy of the laws of the game from this website.

www.6-nations-rugby.com/ sixnations_aboutrugby.htm
The official website of the Six Nations Championship.

www.rfu.com
The official website of the Rugby Football Union.

www.rugby.com.au
A news and information-packed Australian website. Its community section contains short guides for younger players on, for example, techniques, history and mini rugby and other versions of the game.

www.planet-rugby.com
A website with coverage of leagues, cups and national teams from all over the world.

www.rleague.com
The World of Rugby League website has facts, news and profiles from all the main rugby league-playing nations.

Note to parents and teachers: every effort has been made by the Publishers to ensure that these websites are suitable for children, that they are of the highest educational value, and that they contain no inappropriate or offensive material. However, because of the nature of the Internet, it is impossible to guarantee that the contents of these sites will not be altered. We strongly advise that Internet access is supervised by a responsible adult.

Index

22-m line 8, 9

backs 8, 9, 29
ball-carrier 16, 17, 29
ball handling 15
beating an opponent 18–19
Betsen, Serge 21
Botha, Bakkies 27

catching 11, 14–15
centre spot 9
conversion 6, 8, 23, 29
corridor drill 13

dead ball line 8
defence 20–1
drop goals 6, 22, 24, 28
drop kicks 9, 22, 29
dummy pass 18, 29

fitness 11
flankers 8
fly-half 8, 9, 23
forward pass 12, 26, 29
forwards 8, 9, 29
foul play 9
free-kicks 15
full-back 8, 23

garryowens 23
goal kicks 23
goalposts 8
Gordon, Thomas 16
Gough, Ian 27
Gregan, George 26, 28
grubber kicks 23
gumshields 10

halfway line 8
high balls 15
high kicks 23
high tackles 8, 20
history of rugby 6, 7
hooker 8, 26, 27

in-goal areas 6, 8
inside centre 8

kick-offs 9
kicking 22–3
kit 10
knock-on 8, 14, 26, 29

lateral pass 12–13
lineouts 8, 9, 27, 29
lock forwards 8
Lomu, Jonah 11
loose-head prop 8

mark 15
mauls 25
mini rugby 7

Nepia, George 9
No 8 8, 26

Olympics 13
outside centre 8
overlap 16–17, 29

passing 11, 12–13, 18, 19
penalties 8, 12, 15, 25, 27
penalty kicks 6, 8, 23, 24
pitch 8
Poching, Willie 25
points 6, 24, 28
possession 16, 29
protection 10
punts 23

referees 8
restarts 9, 26
rucks 24
rugby league 7, 24, 25, 26,
    28
rugby union 6, 7, 24, 25, 26,
    27, 28
rules 8, 9, 20, 24
runs 16–17

Sailor, Wendell 27
scissors pass 19
scoring 6, 25, 28
scrum caps 10
scrum-half 8, 9, 26, 27
scrums 8, 9, 12, 14, 24, 26,
    29
side-on tackle 20–1
sidestep 11, 19, 29
sin bin 9
skills 11
So'oialo, Steve 9
stand-off 8
stretching exercises 10, 11
supporting runs 16
swerve 11, 18
switch 19

tackling 7, 8, 11, 15, 20–1,
    24–5, 29
tag rugby 7
tap tackle 21, 29
teams 6, 7, 24
throw-ins 27
tight-head prop 8
touch judges 8
touchlines 8, 29
training 10–11
tries 6, 8, 9, 24, 28, 29
try lines 8

up-and-unders 23

video referee 8

Wilkinson, Jonny 22, 28
William Webb Ellis Trophy 6
wingers 8
World Cup 7, 28

30